# MY MIRACLE
## AND LIVING THE GOSPEL
### The Story of Resurection from the Dead

**Rev. Lee Stoneking**

# My MIRACLE
## AND LIVING THE GOSPEL
### The Story of Resurrection from the Dead

My Miracle and Living the Gospel
Unless otherwise indicated, all Scripture quotations are taken from the King James Version of the Bible.

My Miracle and Living the Gospel
ISBN 978-0-615-40748-7
Copyright 2011 by Lee Stoneking

Published by
Lee Stoneking Ministries
www.leestoneking.com

Cover Design and Layout:
Angela Carrington
Inspire Media

Printed in the United States of America.
All rights reserved. No portion of this publication may be reproduced, or transmitted in any form or by any means, electronic, mechanical, photo copy, recording or otherwise, without the prior permission of the author. Brief quotations may be used in literary reviews.

# CONTENTS

| | | |
|---|---|---|
| FOREWORD | | 6 |
| CHAPTER 1 | A FATAL HEART ATTACK! | 9 |
| CHAPTER 2 | EFFORTS TO RESUSCITATE FAIL | 15 |
| CHAPTER 3 | ALIVE! | 19 |
| CHAPTER 4 | THE CHURCH REACTS | 23 |
| CHAPTER 5 | STRUGGLE TO SURVIVE! | 31 |
| CHAPTER 6 | GOD SENDS TWO PRAYER WARRIORS! | 35 |
| CHAPTER 7 | ALIVE AND WITNESSING TO EVERYONE! | 39 |
| CHAPTER 8 | HEADED BACK TO THE UNITED STATES | 45 |
| CHAPTER 9 | MORE MIRACLES! | 49 |
| CHAPTER 10 | PREACHING DURING REST TIME | 55 |
| CHAPTER 11 | EVIDENCE OF MORE MIRACLES | 61 |
| CHAPTER 12 | GOD WRITES THE MUSIC OF OUR LIVES | 65 |
| CHAPTER 13 | SO MUCH KINDNESS! | 75 |
| CHAPTER 14 | OFFICIAL REPORT FROM DOCTOR YOUNG | 79 |
| CHAPTER 15 | FINDINGS FROM DOCTOR WEINER | 85 |
| CHAPTER 16 | MY CONTINUING MINISTRY | 89 |
| CHAPTER 17 | MY MIRACLE CONTINUES | 93 |
| CHAPTER 18 | DOCTOR PITNEY VIEWS MY RECORDS | 103 |
| CHAPTER 19 | 2004 INTERVIEW WITH THE AMBULANCE DRIVER | 107 |
| CHAPTER 20 | THANKS TO THE AUSTRALIAN CHURCH | 113 |
| CHAPTER 21 | RETURN FOR MEDICAL EXAM IN MARCH 2007 | 115 |

# FOREWORD

"Brother Stoneking, I have never known of God to raise a man from the dead to keep preaching the Gospel. God has raised you from the dead to preach the Five-fold Ministry in its fullness. So preach it!"

**T. W. Barnes**

> I SHALL **NOT DIE,**
> BUT **LIVE,**
> AND **DECLARE** THE
> **WORKS** OF THE **LORD.**
> PS 118:17

I WOULD RATHER WALK WITH GOD
IN THE DARKNESS,
THAN GO ALONE IN THE LIGHT.
(MARY BRAINARD)

### Chapter One

# A FATAL HEART ATTACK!

During the second week of November 2003, after preaching an annual crusade for the church in Sydney, Australia, a notable miracle happened to me that changed my life completely.

I had preached that crusade annually for many years. We always experienced marvelous moves of the Holy Ghost! That year the tremendous success of the meeting included fifteen baptized in Jesus' mighty saving name, nine filled with the baptism of the Holy Ghost, and emotional, physical and spiritual healings with miraculous deliverances!

As we looked out over the crowded audiences and experienced the manifestation of the Spirit of God moving mightily in each service to reach one and all, and observed responses from the people we felt excited and uplifted! I am ever so fond of Pastor Slack and the marvelous congregation in Sydney.

MY MIRACLE ~ AND LIVING THE GOSPEL

## *Enjoying the British Influence in Australia*

Since I am half English and enjoy the British culture of the Australian people, I remained in Sydney for a couple of days after the meeting to enjoy the British influence with Pastor Ted Slack and other close friends before leaving for another conference in Hawaii.

On Wednesday Pastor Slack and I left early for the airport so that we could enjoy a late breakfast together before my flight departure. As we had done during previous visits, we again stopped at a favorite kiosk near the security entrance to enjoy parting fellowship. As we stood at the counter ordering, I asked about a certain deletion from an item I wanted to order and then tipped my head back a bit further to look at the very top of the wall menu. That is the last thing I remember until much later when I woke up in the hospital!

## *Experiencing a Fatal Heart Attack*

Later I learned that during that moment I fell instantly dead with a massive heart attack. I did not merely crumple to the floor but instead my body stiffened and fell straight backwards. Consequently, the back of my head landed with tremendous force on the cement floor with a loud cracking noise. Brother Slack told me later, "Brother Stoneking, everyone could hear your head hit the floor! People stopped everything and just watched!"

LEE STONEKING

Exact spot where I fell dead November 12, 2003 Sydney airport on my day of departure.

## *The Prayer of Faith and CPR*

When I struck the floor and Brother Slack realized that I did not respond but appeared to be dead, he dropped to his knees, grabbed hold of me and began praying loudly in my ear, commanding that God raise me from the dead and heal me. Though passing departing crowds gathered to watch, he continued unashamedly to pray commanding in the name of Jesus for His divine intervention. He would not stop praying!

A policeman saw me fall and came running. As soon as he understood the dilemma he took charge and began to administer CPR. He turned to Brother Slack and asked for help,

## MY MIRACLE ~ AND LIVING THE GOSPEL

but Brother Slack responded, "No, I must continue to pray," and Brother Slack continued to compassionately lift my plight to Heaven's Throne.

Soon a second policeman joined the futile, frantic resuscitation attempts but in spite of the surroundings and the commotion, Brother Slack continued to openly intercede for my resurrection from death! I am sure the sight in the airport that day was something for those watching to behold — two policemen frantically struggling with their medical training and rescue techniques alongside the voice of a praying preacher all working over me as I lay dead on the floor.

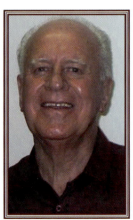

Pastor Slack

WHAT WE DO IN LIFE ECHOES IN ETERNITY

## A TRUE FRIEND

OH THE COMFORT,
THE INEXPRESSIBLE COMFORT
OF FEELING SAFE WITH A PERSON
HAVING NEITHER TO WEIGH
THOUGHTS OR MEASURE WORDS,
BUT POURING THEM OUT
CHAFF AND GRAIN TOGETHER,
SURE THAT A FAITHFUL HAND
WILL TAKE AND SIFT THEM
KEEP WHAT IS WORTH KEEPING
AND WITH THE BREATH OF KINDNESS
BLOW THE REST AWAY

## Chapter Two

# EFFORTS TO RESUSCITATE FAIL

### *Paramedics and Shock Treatments*

Six minutes after I fell, an ambulance arrived on the scene with two men who immediately took over working diligently alongside the policemen. A paramedic arrived soon after. As they came to the conclusion that the CPR attempts were fruitless, they decided to try applying electric shock treatments to my heart. They began by shocking my heart at two hundred joules. No response. They turned up the electricity so that the heart received three hundred sixty joules of electricity and shocked my heart nine times more. Normally this is done only three times before they discontinue the effort of shock treatment. My heart would beat three or four times and then just stop.

Brother Slack told me later, "Brother Stoneking, every time they shocked you, your feet came up off the floor, your head came up off the floor, and then your head would go back down and beat the floor like a jackhammer."

When I heard the story I asked, "Why didn't they put something between my head and the floor?"

He replied, "They were just so concerned about getting your heart to beat that they were not so concerned about some of the *minor* details comparatively speaking." I must confess my head beating the floor like a jackhammer does not strike me as a *minor* detail! As a result I had a very serious concussion!

## *Hopeless — Clinically Dead!*

Nothing the paramedics tried worked. After at least thirty minutes of lying there on the restaurant floor of the airport as they worked to bring me back to life, there was still neither breath nor heartbeat; having exhausted their medical expertise, they gave up. They loaded me into the ambulance and headed for the hospital.

Brother Slack told me later over the phone, "Brother Stoneking, you were dead, dead, dead. Your body felt cold, and your face was covered with cold sweat. Your hair was wet with it. Nothing, absolutely nothing they tried worked, but I continued to pray."

GOD IS NOT SO CONCERNED AS TO WHAT HAPPENS TO US, AS TO HOW WE RESPOND TO WHAT HAPPENS.

WHEN SATAN IS KNOCKING AT YOUR DOOR, SIMPLY SAY, "JESUS, COULD YOU PLEASE GET THAT FOR ME?"

**Chapter Three**

# ALIVE!

## *In the Ambulance — Slated for DOA!*

After they had done everything medically they knew to do, Jesus stepped on the scene. It happened suddenly in the ambulance on the way to the hospital. Since they had given up on me and I had been slated as DOA — dead on arrival — the medical team just stood by. Nigel, the ambulance driver told me the entire story later. On my own without medical assistance of any kind, my heart began to beat and I started to breathe again. This happened after I had been clinically dead for at least 45 minutes! God literally and miraculously resurrected me from the dead. The medical team gaped with astonishment and immediately began to work with me again.

Nigel visited me several times during the stay in the hospital that followed. He could not believe what he had seen and desired to follow up to see what would happen next. One day after I was able to talk with him he said to me, "In all the years I've done ambulance work, I've never seen anything like your experience! I've never seen anyone recover from what happened to you!"

## MY MIRACLE ~ AND LIVING THE GOSPEL

Nigel

I shall ever be most grateful for such burdened and unified efforts on my behalf from each member of the rescue team. May they ever be blessed by God Himself!

### *Hopeless — Clinically Dead!*

Though I was breathing and my heart was beating when I arrived at the hospital I remained unconscious. The doctors in Sydney told everyone who contacted them that I would not live through the week. When my sister called, they said that she could come, but that I would not be alive when she arrived. She came anyway. The doctor's prognosis stated that even if I regained consciousness, I would be brain-dead, unable to speak, unable to walk and with no memory — I would just be a lifeless vegetable. There is good medical reason behind their hopeless prognosis. The fact is that if the brain goes without oxygen for six minutes or more, there is irreparable brain damage.

## *Jesus Had Other Plans!*

The entire medical staff went into a state of shock when I regained consciousness and began to ask questions and make a few simple demands concerning my immediate comfort. They are still in a state of shock! They are not sure what to do with me.

During the time that Jesus walked the shores of Galilee and went about healing the sick and raising the dead, the people of that time were also in a state of shock. They did not know what to do with Him. He still affects the world in this hour with His sovereignty over all. This is the only kind of God I will serve, the only Gospel that I will preach! To be blessed with such a relationship with the Creator Himself, defies human intellect, understanding, and his position of dominion power. Man with his limited knowledge and ability for all time grows strangely dim in the light of His glory and grace! Selah.

## FRIENDS

I ASK ONE THING OF YOU, ONLY ONE, THAT ALWAYS YOU WILL BE MY DREAM OF YOU THAT NEVER SHALL I WAKE TO FIND UNTRUE ALL THIS I HAVE BELIEVED AND RESTED ON FOREVER VANISHED, LIKE A VISION GONE, GONE INTO THE NIGHT.  ALAS! HOW FEW THERE ARE WHO STRIKE IN US A CHORD WE KNEW EXISTED BUT SO SELDOM HEARD ITS TONE, WE TREMBLE AT THE HALF FORGOTTEN SOUND. THE WORLD IS FULL OF RUDE AWAKENINGS AND HEAVEN-BORN CASTLES SHATTERED TO THE GROUND. AND YET OUR HUMAN LONGING VAINLY CLINGS TO A BELIEF IN BEAUTY THROUGH ALL WRONGS;
OH STAY YOUR HAND AND LEAVE MY HEART ITS SONG.

**Chapter Four**

# THE CHURCH REACTS

## *Brother Barnes Is Called*

The following is a letter to me from a precious Australian minister, Brother Richard Nassif, who helped so much during the crisis.

*Dear Brother Stoneking,*

*Just after the doctors said you were still having heart attacks, that they could not do anything for you due to the skull fracture and several blood clots in your heart... We had your phone book from your flight bag and began to phone your close connections – one of them was T. W. Barnes. As soon as I told him the whole situation, he said, "Boy, I am going to pray and then I want you to go and lay your hands on Brother Stoneking, pray and believe for a miracle."*

# MY MIRACLE ~ AND LIVING THE GOSPEL

*The prayer he prayed was the most Authoritative Prayer I have ever witnessed. I felt faith like never before, tears literally shot out of my eyes; an experience that has neither before nor since happened in my lifetime of living for the Lord! He prayed that the Angels of God would surround you and that God would resurrect you from the dead! I have never experienced so much authority from anyone or anywhere. I have traveled to Ethiopia and have been part of several Crusades but nothing as powerful as this!*

*I believe it was a combination of the two; that Brother Barnes had this incredible connection with God and that he loved his Special Son in the Gospel, Lee Stoneking; thus experiencing this incredible authority spoken through the telephone. I now know for all time that the volume of one's voice does not equate to authority flowing from God and His Prophet!*

T.W. Barnes

LEE STONEKING

*We walked back from the front of the hospital into the testing room where there were three other Saints of God present. We did what Brother Barnes said to do despite nurses and doctors surrounding us. Reverend Ron Stevens and I went to the end of the bed and laid hands on it – there was so much authority even though we did not raise our voices – we most assuredly felt God's Powerful Spirit and the Angels of God surrounding your bed.*

*It was only a few minutes later that the many doctors and nurses came together to discuss the action plan. We could hear them talking around us. The doctors had already concluded what they could do with you; the answer was really nothing. It was a period when you were just lying there after they had taken the first pictures of you and your heart condition. They were totally out of options and said to themselves, "There is nothing we can do, we have nothing to lose, let's give it one more chance and take another x-ray of his heart, even though there is blockage in the photo we have. This decision to take another picture was a miracle in itself — this was after the prayer had been prayed by Brother Barnes and myself as he had commanded.* **The rest is history.** *They never have seen this happen. The doctor views 80,000 pictures a year and specifically said, "It just does not change as it did in your case." Praise God!*

Richard Nassif

MY MIRACLE ~ AND LIVING THE GOSPEL

## Switchboards Jammed

I remember hearing various reports once I regained consciousness and after my release from the Sydney hospital regarding the initial inquiries made concerning my condition.

With the news of my heart attack spreading across our fellowship, which covers the world, phone calls came in to the Sydney, Australia hospital requesting information and updates. This jammed the hospital switchboards with more calls than they were able to handle. They felt frustrated not only because of the number of calls, but since the staff felt perplexed at my continually changing condition, they were unable to explain this to the many callers jamming the switchboards. A common question was repeated as the caller was placed on hold, "What do I tell them?"

The hospital staff said, "We don't know who this man is but we cannot handle the number of calls coming in with questions regarding his condition."

Similar problems occurred at our church headquarters building in St. Louis. It took a few days before the staff could find ways to handle the number of inquiries that came through the switchboard there.

The same thing happened when I returned to the United States and was placed in the hospital in Jackson, Tennessee.

All of these phone calls and inquiries created quite a stir and later someone related to me a most interesting comment from my stay in the Sydney hospital. In spite of the tubes, wires, breathing apparatus, oxygen equipment, and somewhat shocking discolorations and bruises on my very swollen face, they said, "He is a distinguished looking man. He must be someone of importance." I am someone of importance – I am an Ambassador of King Jesus!

## *Two Thumbs Up!*

Some very interesting sideline events, that I have no conscious memory of, have been since related to me as I have worked to obtain a panoramic picture of my miracle of recovery and return to life. During my return trip to Sydney one year later I heard many stories that helped me piece the entire picture together.

Brother Richard Nassif from Australia relates that while I lay in the hospital bed in what appeared to be a comatose state, virtually lifeless, he looked at me, felt badly and decided to do something for me. So he got up and walking over to the foot of the bed, gently rolled back the blanket and began to massage my feet and ankles. He looked at me and asked, "Do you like that?" In spite of the seeming comatose state, I pulled both hands out from under the covers and gave him two thumbs up. It was some of the first positive response that they had gotten from me. In view of the doctor's prognosis Richard and those in the room were shocked but chuckled as they watched me and felt the comforting assurance of the presence of God feeling certain from that moment on that I would make it.

## *Visitation of Angels*

Many people who visited me expressed that upon entering the room they saw angels standing near me and/or hovering over me. More than one report came that said they saw an angel hovering over me near the ceiling. What a mighty God we serve! It is written that:

> *The angel of the Lord encampeth round about them that fear Him, and delivereth them (Psalm 34:7).*

His laws are immutable, unchanging, perfect, and He is the guiding Light of all those who know Him and call Him Lord!

WRITE YOUR NAME IN KINDNESS, LOVE, AND MERCY ON THE HEARTS OF THE THOUSANDS YOU MEET, AND IT WILL BECOME AN INDELIBLE MASTERPIECE NONE CAN EVER FORGET!

I SHALL PASS THROUGH
THIS WORLD BUT ONCE.
IF, THEREFORE, THERE BE ANY
KINDNESS I CAN SHOW, OR ANY GOOD
THING I CAN DO, LET ME DO IT NOW;
LET ME NOT DEFER IT NOR NEGLECT IT,
FOR I SHALL NOT PASS THIS WAY AGAIN.

## Chapter Five

# STRUGGLE TO SURVIVE!

## *Struggle with Tubes and Wires*

Apparently the medical team assisting me felt quite baffled and struggled to know how to administer treatment. They diagnosed the initial problem as a massive heart attack. Subsequent problems occurred because of the concussion received from the fall and from my head hammering the floor during the ten electric shock treatments. To administer blood thinner medications to treat the heart would complicate the problems with the severe concussion. They felt that their only chance of seeing me recover would be if they could keep me quiet long enough for the concussion to stop bleeding and begin to heal. Faint hopes of success kept them working to conquer the problems with the concussion so that they could then begin to administer effective treatment for the heart. Keeping me alive while they helped to facilitate that process remained a challenge — one which I am sure they really wondered if they would succeed in accomplishing.

Even though I remained somewhat unconscious they administered heavy sedatives to keep me still so that the bleeding would stop and I would begin to heal. At times it must have become difficult to decipher whether I remained unconscious or just heavily sedated. The results appeared similar. To keep me alive and administer the medications necessary they hooked up a tangled mess of tubes and wires through the nose, mouth and throat.

Even in my heavily sedated state, the tubes and wires irritated me to the point that I would pull them out of their placement. Later they explained to me that I would consistently pull them out whenever I could; however, to my chagrin, they simply replaced them with even larger ones. The new ones must have irritated me even more because I would immediately attempt to remove them as well. The nurses constantly ran back and forth conferring with one another and dutifully replacing the removed tubes and wires. They felt exasperated and understandably so!

Later I asked, "Brother Slack, how was I really?"

He said, "You were terrible boy, you were terrible."

I replied, "I don't remember that."

He said, "Well, you wouldn't because they gave you so many drugs." I have since learned that it is common practice to give the patient drugs to destroy short term memory so that the pain and trauma incurred are not remembered.

Finally the hospital staff devised an apparatus which they felt quite confident would prevent my arms and hands from breaking free to pull out the tubes and wires. They felt some pride in their invention and felt sure they had come up with the solution. My sister, who watched as they proudly installed the apparatus, told me all about it later. When they had finished they confidently left the room feeling sure that this time they had the problem solved. Within minutes my hands had broken free, I had pulled out the tubes and wires again and standing to my feet, I demanded my suitcases declaring that I was going home! I do not remember this.

YOU'RE HERE NOT BY CHANCE,
BUT BY GOD'S CHOOSING.
HIS HAND FORMED YOU AND
MADE YOU THE PERSON YOU ARE.
HE COMPARES YOU TO NO ONE ELSE –
YOU ARE ONE OF A KIND.
YOU LACK NOTHING THAT
HIS GRACE CAN'T GIVE YOU.
HE HAS ALLOWED YOU TO BE HERE
AT THIS TIME IN HISTORY
TO FULFILL HIS SPECIAL PURPOSE
FOR THIS GENERATION.

### Chapter Six

## GOD SENDS
## TWO PRAYER WARRIORS!

### *Brother Young and Brother Doug*

Within five days of being admitted to the hospital, Pastor Jeff Young and Doug, a member of his church in Bethel Springs, Tennessee, came to my side and together they also witnessed my ongoing struggle with the tubes and wires.

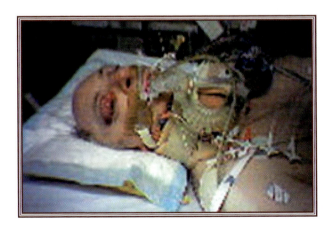

## MY MIRACLE ~ AND LIVING THE GOSPEL

That first morning that they were there the doctors and nurses came into my room and boldly declared (because they were so exasperated with me) "We are going to totally strap him down so he cannot move his hands and arms at all."

Brother Young stood to his feet and said, "No, we will not allow you to do that to him. We will sit with him all day long, and when he tries to move his hands or arms to pull the tubes out, we will hold him down and pray." The doctors just looked at them and then turned and walked out. Throughout that day, every time I tried to move, they gripped my arms and held them down praying for me in Jesus' all-powerful name. They operated in this manner of burden and caring for me the entire day. That is an example of living the Gospel — executing the power of God that is within us as believers! Amen!

Brother Doug and Pastor Young

# LEE STONEKING

The next morning, when Brother Young and Brother Doug walked into my room to once again minister to me as necessary, they found me sitting up on the side of my bed! Looking at them I asked, "Brother Young, what are you doing here?" It was the first time I actually realized that they were there.

At about the same time the doctor walked in looking at me and said, "This is not the same man I treated last night." Their prayers had broken the effect of the drugs and had brought healing to my body! From that day on I was restored to normal! Their prayers had been marvelously answered! The Lord be praised! The news spread through the hospital!

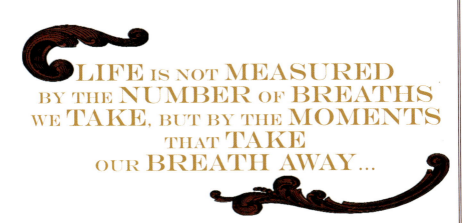

LIFE IS NOT MEASURED BY THE NUMBER OF BREATHS WE TAKE, BUT BY THE MOMENTS THAT TAKE OUR BREATH AWAY...

MY WORLD
THE CIRCLE OF GOD'S WILL

MY SUN AND MOON
HIS FACE

DARKNESS
THE SHADOW OF HIS WING

RAIN
HIS REFRESHING GRACE

MY FOOD
HIS EVERLASTING WORD

MY PASTURES GREEN
HIS LOVE

MUSIC
HIS VOICE WITHIN MY HEART

MY HOME
WITH HIM ABOVE

## Chapter Seven

# ALIVE AND WITNESSING TO EVERYONE!

### *Trying to Explain the Sudden Change*

God sent people to be by my side that would watch over me. Saints from the Sydney church took turns coming to be with me throughout those hospitalized days. They stayed from early morning until late each night. I later learned of their kindness and shall never forget their acts of caring and love!

As the news spread throughout the hospital that I had been restored to normal, some of the staff came into my room simply stating, "The doctors want to talk with you."

I said, "Fine." Two doctors came in and sat down in chairs at the foot of my bed not saying one word to me but just stared at the floor. Because they did not say anything, I felt badly and thought to myself, I must not be cooperating. There's something I am not doing. Consequently I said, "Gentleman, I am sorry if I am not cooperating with you. I want to cooperate with you, but I did not sleep well last night, I have a headache,

MY MIRACLE ~ AND LIVING THE GOSPEL

and I do not really feel all that well"—an understatement to say the least in view of the death experience I had just been through!

One of the doctors replied, "Reverend, it has nothing to do with you personally."

I raised my head up slightly from my pillow and lying position to ask, "What then does it have to do with?"

The doctor responded with a sound of puzzlement in his voice, "Medically, you should be dead but you are not and we do not know why."

I responded by asking, "Have you ever heard of Christ Jesus from Nazareth?" They neither answered me nor did they look me directly in the face but only glanced at me and then quickly looked away and continued to stare at the floor; so I posed the question a second time, more emphatically, "Have either of you ever heard of this man Christ Jesus from Nazareth?"

One of the doctors looked directly at me and said, "Yes, we have heard of Him."

I said, "So, you both admit that you know about Him?"

They both answered "Yes."

I said, "Here is understanding for you: You know *about* Him, *but I know Him!*"

# LEE STONEKING

Both doctors became visibly and emotionally moved! I shall never forget the presence of God we felt in those few moments of time. Jesus captured our immediate attention.

From that moment on, the news continued spreading throughout the hospital! Complete strangers visited my room — politely coming and going to view the phenomenon. Nurses and doctors came just to look at me. Most of them did not talk to me. They just came to look — it felt most unusual. As I lay there in bed, people simply came to the door, looked for varied lengths of time, and then went away. While some of them spoke a little, many just wanted to hear me tell what Jesus had done for me. I did not always feel like talking, but I decided that as long as they wanted to hear, I would tell them of His Great Power. I decided that I would speak of Him even if I perished in the process.

## *Grotesque Facial Appearance*

To understand the true scenario let me explain what I looked like. I looked terrible! My face and eyes had become grotesquely swollen because of the tremendous impact with which my head repeatedly hit the cement floor during the initial fall and during the ten electric shock treatments to my heart. Because the back of my head pounded the floor again and again like a jackhammer each time they administered a treatment with the electricity hitting my body, it forced the blood to come to the front of my head and surface on the face just under the skin turning the colors from my natural skin color to black, blue, red, and purple. I looked terribly awful! However, those who came

# MY MIRACLE ~ AND LIVING THE GOSPEL

to my door to view me didn't seem to mind what I looked like! They just wanted to hear what I had to say!

This served as a powerful reminder that this world does not care so much what we look like, they just want to hear what we have to say about Jesus. They want to know if He is real and if He lives powerfully now among us as He did 2000 years ago.

**Lesson learned:**
*Let us kill the pride within us as fellow Christian believers and march onward with the shining glow of God's holiness and purity. To this end were you born again that you might convey to a world lost in darkness His glorious light and ways. You are a light, a city set on a hill that cannot be hid!*

## *Patient Serves Tea and Baklava to the Staff*

One night late I woke up and seeing a large package of one of my favorite Middle Eastern pastries, baklava, which friends from the church had brought, I suddenly decided to do something. The hospital staff constantly served others — I would serve them. I got up and walked down to the nurses' station. I made my announcement that it was time they had a break with my compliments of hot tea and pastries for each of them...

Possibly it was one of the most unusual things that the hospital staff had ever experienced from a patient; because at first they just stared at me with shocked looks on their faces.

Then they began to smile and to show appreciation as they allowed me to serve them and as they enjoyed the tea along with my sweet offerings.

Many of the details have been forgotten because of the trauma and the medications; however, my English heritage and personality made its contribution that night in the form of gracious British hospitality. In that disciplined hospital setting this caused quite a stir especially as it came from a somewhat difficult patient who had miraculously recovered overnight! I am quite sure the event will not soon be forgotten.

IT IS WHEN WE
FORGET OURSELVES
THAT WE DO THINGS
THAT ARE REMEMBERED!!!

GOD DOESN'T CALL THE QUALIFIED,
HE QUALIFIES THE CALLED.

## Chapter Eight

# HEADED BACK TO THE UNITED STATES

### *Released and Back to the Airport*

After fourteen days they released me from the hospital in Sydney, Australia. As I left the doctors transmitted friendship and genuine appreciation for me personally with best wishes for my future.

Upon leaving the hospital, I stayed with wonderful friends from the Sydney church, the Grech family, for six days more to make sure I would be able to travel back to the United States. During my stay in their home the blessings of the Lord flowed. Church members brought in food and we shared precious fellowship continually laced with prayer and personal burden support.

I am told that during that week I helped with suggestions in further decorating the Grech's home – though I do not remember this with much clarity. We have chuckled over the details more than once.

MY MIRACLE ~ AND LIVING THE GOSPEL

At the end of this pleasant restoring experience, once again Pastor Slack drove me to the airport. We entered the restaurant where it all happened and as we walked through the door, those that worked there recognized me and remembering what had happened they became emotional and tearful as we recounted together the details of my miracle of resurrection from the dead given at the hands of the Master!

THE HELP CAME
FROM THE LORD,
BUT THE HELPING HANDS
WERE YOURS.
THANK YOU!

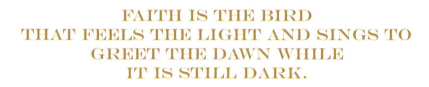

FAITH IS THE BIRD
THAT FEELS THE LIGHT AND SINGS TO
GREET THE DAWN WHILE
IT IS STILL DARK.

### Chapter Nine

## MORE MIRACLES!

### *Jackson, Tennessee Hospital*

My medical records from Sydney, Australia preceded me to the hospital in Jackson, Tennessee where Brother Young's son, Jeff is a heart specialist. Leaving Sydney, I flew over thirty hours straight through to Memphis, Tennessee. The Youngs met me at the airport and drove me to Bethel Springs where I stayed overnight in their lovely home.

The following day they took me to the hospital in Jackson, Tennessee where they introduced me to a brilliant heart specialist, Dr. Weiner. He placed me on an operating table to examine my heart and consider treatment; but after reviewing the records sent from Sydney he said to me, "Reverend, we cannot do anything for your heart due to the damage caused by the concussion. Your skull is fractured, and there are large pools of blood seepage on either side of your brain in the back of your head. If we give you any kind of anticoagulant we could lose you on the table."

## MY MIRACLE ~ AND LIVING THE GOSPEL

# *A Miracle and a New Set of Head X-rays*

I had seen my head x-rays earlier and knew the truth concerning the fracture and blood seepage pools. So I said "Well, we will pray!" We did and then they took another set of pictures.

Shortly after the second set of pictures were taken, the doctor came back into the room shaking his head and saying, "You are the most unusual patient we have ever had in this hospital. This makes no sense at all."

I asked, "What do you mean?"

He said, "There is no fracture in the skull, and there is no blood seepage in the brain. There is no evidence that you've even had a concussion." All we can find is a small scar. You must have gotten hit in the head when you were a child." Immediately after that I was taken to the operating room where Dr. Weiner inserted stents into the narrowed vein which facilitated the heart attack on the right side of my heart.

The unspoken truth felt in the human spirit realm basically screamed, "If we didn't have the x-rays and the photos from Sydney, we would believe they had misdiagnosed you! But, we cannot deny the photographs that we have." It was another miracle in the rapid succession of miracles on my behalf! Somewhere between the time of their prognosis/diagnosis and the time it took to make a second set of photos, Jesus once again stepped on the scene and applied His touch of immediate miraculous healing! It was another miracle! Oh what a Savior!

LEE STONEKING

## *The Miracle of My Vision*

The doctors told me that it was a very real possibility that I would lose some or, in the worst scenario, all of my vision! They explained that this fear came from the tremendous trauma caused by the impact of my head beating the cement floor! It is not unusual in similar situations for the retinas in both eyes to be seriously damaged! So when I returned home I made an appointment and went to my eye doctor and told him the whole story.

The doctor felt so compassionately moved by my testimony of God's power that he just sat there shaking his head! Finally he said, "I am not even going to charge you. I have never heard anything like this!" After he examined my eyes, he told me that my field of vision was totally intact.

"The trauma you suffered should have diminished your field of vision because of damage to the cerebral cortex – posterior or 'occipital' cortex, also known as the 'visual cortex' – but the retinas were not damaged!" To God be the glory! AMEN.

## MY MIRACLE ~ AND LIVING THE GOSPEL

### *Listed as the "Miracle Patient"*

God continued to astound the doctors and me. Dr. Young explained, "It takes at least six months for the muscles of the heart to even begin to function normally after an attack like you've had. But from the moment you regained consciousness, they began to function normally! It is as if you never had a heart attack!"

Other doctors involved with my case also expressed their astonishment. They said, "You have defied all of the laws of medical science."

My response as I pointed upward was, "I didn't, but I know the One who did!" I am listed as a miracle patient in both the American and Sydney hospitals.

### *Not One Second of Fear*

In spite of the sudden heart attack, the long hospital stay, the medical experts foretelling information that sounded so negative — the entire diagnosis and prognosis, I never had one second of fear! This in itself is amazing and very wonderful.

I have had the Holy Ghost, been baptized in Jesus name, lived for Him and preached this Gospel for over forty-six years and since having been held in the cold lifeless hands of death, I find that it is definitely true — there is no fear in death! We have told people who are born into the Kingdom of God, that to be absent from the body is to be present with the Lord — that it is better to go to heaven and be with Jesus than to abide here.

# LEE STONEKING

The reason I never had a single moment of fear is because I have nothing to be afraid of! My sufficiency is totally in Him. I am ready to go, I am ready to stay — whatever His bidding may be. What a marvelous way to live and what incredible comfort to possess! Simply stated: IT IS FREEDOM that only Jesus can give!

I have traveled much of the world, prayed for dead people and life came into their bodies again! I have been eye witness to thousands receiving the Holy Ghost! I have seen legs grow in length to match the other leg, blind eyes opened, deaf ears unstopped, tumors and cysts disappear, cancers melt away, and literally all manner of diseases healed by the dear and Glorious Physician — Jesus! We have nothing to fear except fear itself! This Jesus we serve can do anything! You do remember: He made a body out of clay — He can repair it!

YOU HAVE TO DECIDE;
DO YOU WANT TO CONTROL DOZENS
OR DO YOU WANT TO LEAD THOUSANDS?

### Chapter Ten

# PREACHING DURING REST TIME

## *Just Be Seated Among the People*

When the doctors released me from the hospital I heard them say, "You cannot travel for six months."

I replied, "No, I can't do that."

Finally, after some negotiating they agreed, "Then two months of rest with no travel?"

I replied, "I can do that." The doctors seemed content with my two month compliance.

So it was that during January and February of 2004 I planned to be home recovering from the trauma of a massive heart attack, clinical death pronouncement lasting 45 minutes, concussion, miraculous healing of blood seepage on the brain, and becoming acquainted with the resurrection power that was very present in my life.

## MY MIRACLE ~ AND LIVING THE GOSPEL

For many years during the latter part of January, I have preached the last night of Landmark Convention that is held in Stockton, California. Though I had dutifully cancelled all of my commitments for January and February, during the time that I rested Brother Haney phoned me and asked, "Brother Stoneking, is it possible that you could just fly to Stockton and be seated among the people on Friday night of Landmark while I preach so that they can see you? It would be such a blessing to the entire conference on the last night!"

I answered, "I think I could do that. I am not supposed to be traveling, but I could do that much." So it was arranged. I arrived on Thursday afternoon before the final service of Landmark the next evening. Nathaniel Haney picked me up at the Sacramento airport and we enjoyed the fellowship of the powerful, miraculous setting surrounding my life!

Brother and Sister Kenneth Haney called Friday morning inviting me to have lunch with them. I was most happy to accept. When they arrived at my hotel, I walked out and met them. They both said almost simultaneously, "You look wonderful!" I thanked the Lord and them!

It felt delightful to see my longtime friends and while seated in the restaurant, Brother Haney related the message he planned to preach that night. He entitled it, *What Is the Church?* Contents: The church is not a social gathering, it is not a club, it is the House of God where people repent, are saved, delivered, healed, set free, and are *raised from the dead*!

It sounded wonderful in content and I could feel the expectancy and God's Spirit moving as he concluded the thoughts from his message.

And then he asked, "Is it possible that you could just finish the last ten minutes of my message tonight?"

I said, "I think I can do that." And it was agreed.

They purposely scheduled me to arrive about 15 minutes after the service had begun so that I could be brought in quietly from a side door and seated quickly on the end of the front row facing the platform and pulpit. For that reason most of the 6,000 people in attendance did not see me come in to the service. Most were not aware that I was there—just those on my immediate left side of the front knew and saw me.

As Brother Haney preached his last words telling of the church—a place of healing, deliverance, and *where people are raised from the dead*, he walked down from the platform and came directly to me. When he did, I stood and receiving the microphone began walking to the platform. The people realized I was there alive! They were viewing a miracle of God in which they had participated with prayerful weeping, intercessions in the Spirit of God lifting their faith to His Throne. They began to clap and applaud. It was a standing ovation! A moving experience that is ever with me!

# My Miracle ~ and Living the Gospel

For the next eight to ten minutes the anointing and power of God hit me! With a spirit of resurrection power and witness I proclaimed His power and truth. Miracles took place throughout the audience with people coming to the altar area in great numbers. They came to the edge of the platform which is about five feet above the floor and reached for me. I did not leave the platform for concern of getting overwhelmed with the needs and crowd in general but rather bent low toward all of them along the edge, laying hands on as many as I could reach out to and touch.

I was doing well and felt the power of God to minister; however, Brother Haney came up behind me and said, "Brother Stoneking, you are doing too much."

I said, "No, I am all right." He walked away.

About ten minutes later he came again and said, "Brother Stoneking, you are overdoing it!"

I said, "No, I am still doing fine." He walked away.

About six minutes later three ushers came and said, "We are taking you out of the sanctuary at Brother Haney's orders." Thus ended my altar work at Landmark 2004!

The doctors never knew about this "just being seated in the audience" experience and my ministering before the two months of rest had been completed.

It was a glorious experience for me and obviously for all present.  God so mightily moved with healing and miracles throughout the crowd.  One older man, who had suffered with a heart condition, met me outside on the parking lot as I moved toward my vehicle of exit.  He came running across the parking lot shouting, "Brother Stoneking, I am healed of my heart condition!  I can run with no pain!"  He grabbed me and we worshipped together in among the cars.  Numbers of other testimonies of healing from that service could be told here.

PEOPLE MAY NOT REMEMBER EXACTLY WHAT YOU DID OR WHAT YOU SAID, BUT THEY WILL ALWAYS REMEMBER HOW YOU MADE THEM FEEL.

## Chapter Eleven

# EVIDENCE OF MORE MIRACLES

## *Back to the Hospital Four Months Later*

In March of 2004, I preached a crusade for Dr. Young's parents. At the end of the crusade, I went back to the hospital in Jackson, Tennessee just so they could check the status of my healed and raised-from-the-dead heart. It had been arranged in December of 2003 for me to return for checkup and perhaps add more stents on the left side of the heart in view of the fact that Dr. Weiner had noted two narrow places in the arteries on that side. Dr. Weiner had stated that he was going to fix everything that could be fixed. His reasoning: if I traveled only in the United States there would be no concern but since I was out of the country a great deal, we needed to do all that we could to ensure my health and safety.

Upon arriving at the hospital, I lay down on the operating table wide awake! Dr. Weiner did his initial examination, began making the corrections to the left side of the heart and checked the muscle where the heart attack actually hit. "I want to see how that muscle is doing," he commented.

# MY MIRACLE ~ AND LIVING THE GOSPEL

I watched some of the procedure on the monitor next to me as Dr. Weiner executed his examination of my heart. Suddenly he stopped working and just stared straight ahead. After a few seconds, he turned and walked around the glass partition separating us and looked down at me. With a look of amazement upon his face, his eyes made contact with my own lying there on the table and he solemnly proclaimed, "The Lord is with you."

I said, "What do you mean?"

He answered, "That muscle has totally, totally recovered! It's as if you never had a heart attack."

That is a medical impossibility! We know it and the doctors know it. They have no choice at this point but to admit that divine intervention has come from God on my behalf. The miracles have completely exceeded and overridden their medical expertise, training, and knowledge. May it ever be noted, recognized, and proclaimed that: every miracle begins with impossibility and that the physician of all physicians is the Creator Himself!

THOSE WHO KNEEL BEFORE GOD, CAN STAND BEFORE ANYONE...

**IF THE DEVIL CANNOT STEAL YOUR JOY,
HE CANNOT KEEP YOUR GOODS!**

## Chapter Twelve

# GOD WRITES
# THE MUSIC OF OUR LIVES

I am persuaded that Jesus knew exactly what He was doing when He left me clinically dead for 45 minutes or more. I believe He did it purposely in order to defy all the laws of medical science. The profound truth of God's dealing with humanity brought to life anew and afresh during this time of reflection is this:

*Not without design does God write the music of our lives. Be it ours to learn the time and not to be discouraged at the rests.*

What would great music be without the timing and the rests? The beauty of the melody, and the emotion of its purpose would be distorted with the impact lost upon its hearer without the timing and the rests! God's music has a way of plucking from our very nerve fiber and heart strings that which will thrill the hearer with hope, victory, and joy.

MY MIRACLE ~ AND LIVING THE GOSPEL

## *When You Were Dead Did You See Anything?*

Many preachers from all over the world called me in the early months of my recovery and return to life. Several of them asked me this question. "Brother Stoneking, when you were dead, did you see anything?"

And my answer is this: "No, no, no! I did not see anything at all. Jesus knows me too well for that. If I had seen Him, talked with Him, seen the Holy City or the angels, there is no way I would have come back. I would have pushed to stay with Him. There is no way I would have come back to this world!"

Jesus knows me – we have been the closest of friends for over 46 years. Obviously His work for me in the world's field of harvest before His soon return is not finished. I labor gladly ministering to any and all with great burden to transmit His reality, greatness, and mercy which as David of old sang — his mercy endureth forever!

## *Jesus Is the Resurrection and the Life!*

Looking back on everything Jesus has done for me, I believe He allowed me to be raised from the dead so that I would understand this fact: the Jesus I read about in Scripture is just as alive and able today as He was two thousand years ago.

He has not changed! This is not some fairytale story, but this is reality. He is real! He can cause the lame to walk, the blind to see, the deaf to hear, and the dead to be raised to life again! I know firsthand that He is the Resurrection and the Life!

As never before, I can relate to Lazarus as he walked out of the tomb of death. Only Jesus can demand we return from that exit of life, from that valley of darkness into the light of His presence and back to life here on earth. To God be the glory! Amen forever!

He can take away cancer, cause legs to grow, heal and change a mind and cause a body to be made whole from any sickness and even from death! He not only allows all of this to happen in order to manifest Himself in such Biblical miraculous ways, but He has also allowed it to happen to convince us as a people that He wants to do the supernatural among us. He longs to do the miraculous in and through us!

## *Apostolic Christianity*

There are many kinds of Christianity in the world today created by man with his misguided understandings from among his own peers and within the human framework of intellect, fleshly desires, and reasoning. However, there is only one kind of Christianity that God recognizes and that is the Christianity He began Himself in 33 AD in an upper room in Old Jerusalem.

With the sound of the rushing mighty wind, cloven tongues of fire sat upon the heads of believers as they were born again. The Spirit cried from within signifying that He had taken up His residence in the heart and soul of human flesh! This is the ultimate goal of the Creator. The second chapter of the book of Acts records the miraculous and triumphant birth of the church.

MY MIRACLE ~ AND LIVING THE GOSPEL

Just as sound accompanies natural birth with a baby crying, so birth of the Spirit of God in us is accompanied by the Spirit crying from within as He takes up residence in our souls! (Acts 2)

God's ultimate desire from the beginning of time is not to sit upon a mountain top as with the giving of the Law under Moses, but rather to make His ostentatious entrance of residence into our lives as He did at the advent of Pentecost in 33 AD when fire rested upon the heads of men and women as He took up residence in their hearts.

Fire and wind accompanied the inauguration of the Law written in stone at Sinai in the Old Testament. In the New Testament fire and wind also accompanied the inauguration of the Law of God being written in the heart and flesh of man!

Jesus had promised, "I am with you, but I shall be in you." God overshadowed Mary to mix flesh with God. God gave the Holy Ghost to mix God with flesh! That is exactly what takes place when we become true Bible believers. Because of this miracle of Christ living in us, Mark records the words of Jesus saying:

*These signs shall follow them that believe; in my Name shall they cast out devils; they shall speak with new tongues; they shall take up serpents; and if they drink any deadly thing, it shall not hurt them; they shall lay hands on the sick and they shall recover (Mark 16:17-18).*

# He died that I might live!

### And I am alive because of His Death, His Life, His Love, and His Mercy!

# To God Be The Glory!

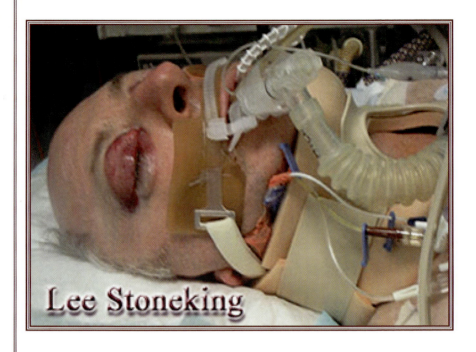

Most people in my condition are dead
when they arrive at the hospital.

# I was not!

*There is only one reason for that ...*

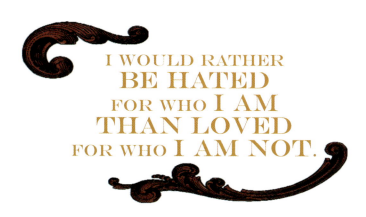

# MY MIRACLE ~ AND LIVING THE GOSPEL

## *A Strong Desire to Be Used by God*

During the three years I attended Apostolic Bible Institute in St Paul, Minnesota, each day we were given a fifteen minute break time. I neither went downstairs to play ping pong nor ate donuts during that time, but rather went to the prayer room and there I daily pleaded with God to use my life.

I begged Him to use my life so that my living would not be in vain — that I would not just occupy space on planet earth. When God answers prayers like these, it comes with His specifications, His needs, His qualifications, and His desires — rarely does it look like what we had pictured in the theater of our mind's eye. The things that happen to us many times are nothing more or nothing less than the shadow of His hand outstretched caressingly. He is never so near as when we think He is so far away. This has never been as evident in my life as it is at this time.

Faith is simply: *BLINDLY TRUSTING THAT GOD WILL ALWAYS DO THAT WHICH IS RIGHT BY US.* The more we think about this powerful statement with meditation and deepening thought, the more we understand how simple but true it is.

THE ONLY THING WE OWN IN THIS WORLD ARE THE CHOICES WE MAKE

FRIENDS ARE ANGELS
WHO LIFT US TO OUR FEET
WHEN OUR WINGS HAVE TROUBLE
REMEMBERING HOW TO FLY

### Chapter Thirteen

## SO MUCH KINDNESS!

### *Many Loved Ones Supported Me*

Immediately upon hearing of my falling dead with a massive heart attack in Sydney, Pastor Jeff Young Sr. from Bethel Springs, Tennessee caught the first plane to Sydney to be by my side along with Brother Doug from his congregation. My sister made the tremendous sacrifice to travel all that distance and arrived as soon as she could. Others also traveled great distances to be near. There is no way to explain the love, comfort, peace, and security their presence and their prayers brought to me personally. It means more than words can say!

In addition to those from out of the country, a large group of saints from Australia itself loved and supported me through this trauma. The support I felt from the saints and friends from the church in Sydney was totally beyond the call of duty in every way. Their kindness and help is rated among some of the very highest in all of my life's experiences. To say that I am completely indebted is an understatement. I shall never forget their kindnesses!

# MY MIRACLE ~ AND LIVING THE GOSPEL

The homes opened and hospitality given me in both countries brought to me a whole new understanding and perspective of what Christianity really entails. To experience it in the manner which I did allowed me to experience Christianity from the first church in its beginning as it is described in the book of Acts.

I am most thankful for all that has happened to me. The time spent in hospitals among people both known and unknown to me has caused a re-evaluation of life and ministry.

THE GOOD YOU FIND IN OTHERS IS IN YOU TOO

FEAR IS THE DARK ROOM
WHERE SATAN DEVELOPS
HIS PICTURES IN OUR LIVES

## Chapter Fourteen

# OFFICIAL REPORT FROM DOCTOR YOUNG

Dr. Jeff Young Jr.
Dr. Young is expertise personified—
He is brilliant and totally professional in his field!

Official Medical Report: On November 12, 2003, Reverend Stoneking suffered a cardiac arrest due to a massive heart attack. He suffered this ventricular fibrillation arrest at the airport in Sydney, Australia.

# MY MIRACLE ~ AND LIVING THE GOSPEL

Ventricular fibrillation (VF) is the most commonly identified arrhythmia in cardiac arrest patients. This arrhythmia is a severe derangement of the heartbeat that usually ends in death within minutes unless corrective measures are promptly taken. Cardiopulmonary resuscitation (CPR) was administered by bystanders until paramedics could arrive. I quote a letter I received from Dr. Mark Pitney in Australia *(Brother Stoneking's attending physician while in the hospital overseas)*: "Even with intubation *(a breathing tube in place)*, paramedic CPR and repeated cardio versions *(shocks to the heart—ten total shocks!)*, a stable rhythm *(heartbeat)* and output *(circulation)* was not gained for thirty minutes." Basically, in common everyday vernacular, Brother Stoneking was dead for thirty minutes. The first miracle of this was that he lived at all. Sudden cardiac death accounts for approximately 300,000 deaths per year in the United States, of which 75-80% is due to VF. More deaths are attributable to VF than to lung cancer, breast cancer, or AIDS. A major adverse outcome from a VF event is anoxic encephalopathy *(brain damage due to lack of oxygen)*, which occurs in 30-80% of patients.

Irreversible brain damage usually occurs within 6 minutes. Again, according to Brother Stoneking's reports and the doctors I spoke with directly in Australia, no adequate heartbeat or circulation was established for thirty minutes. When he collapsed, he struck his head on the concrete floor causing large hematomas. As if a heart attack and VF arrest were not enough, this was a terribly complicating set of events. A hematoma is a localized mass of blood confined within a space. So when he fell he developed blood on the brain.

# LEE STONEKING

The reason this complicates matters so, is that the number one treatment for a patient having a heart attack is the use of powerful blood thinners. Since he had bleeding on the brain he could not undergo any treatment for his heart attack. Also, the fall caused a fracture of his skull. He was taken to the cardiac catheterization lab *(a special procedure room used to take angiograms or pictures of the arteries of the heart)*. There they "initially" felt he needed to have open-heart surgery. However, when I spoke with Dr. Pitney he stated to me, "I will send you Mr. Stoneking's films for you and your colleagues to look at because I can't explain what happened between the first shot and the second shot!" What he meant by this was, with the first pictures taken it looked as though Brother Stoneking would need three to four bypasses because it looked like he had several severe blockages. However, in the very next picture his blockages looked better. Because of this miraculous finding, as well as, a spontaneous and what I can only explain as miraculous resolution of his heart attack, it was felt by his neurologist and cardiologist in Sydney that he could be stabilized and sent back to the states for any procedures he might require. Miraculously, and that is the only words I can use because it is a miracle, Brother Stoneking recovered in Sydney without any brain damage. Upon getting him back to the states we readmitted him to the hospital and my colleagues and I began our own work-up. The MRI of his brain here miraculously showed "no evidence of bleeding or even prior bleeding." This is a documented miracle, because I have a CT scan report from Australia that shows blood on the brain. We also did a repeat CT scan after the MRI results to better assess his skull fracture. I was in the CT room with Brother Stoneking and the radiologist

# MY MIRACLE ~ AND LIVING THE GOSPEL

kept getting more and more pictures and questioned me about whether the doctors in Sydney were correct about the skull fracture because the only fracture he could find on CT here was one that looked "old." This was another miracle!! Brother Stoneking finally underwent successful balloon angioplasty and stent to a 100% blocked right coronary artery. The final miracle of it all was discovered in our Cath Lab here in the states. Brother Stoneking's heart was functioning at about half of what it should. As a result of this he had some fluid on his lungs in Australia, a common complication following a heart attack of this magnitude. With any heart attack there is usually some residual damage and this can be indefinite and can take up to 6 months for stunned myocardium *(heart muscle)* to recover, if it recovers at all. When we reassessed his heart function here, his heart function was entirely normal!!! I can truly say that Brother Stoneking's recovery and medical course is miraculous. He was nicknamed the "miracle patient" at our hospital and people would come by just to see and talk with him. To God be the glory!! God is still in the miracle working business in the 21st century!

*Dr. Jeff Young Jr.*

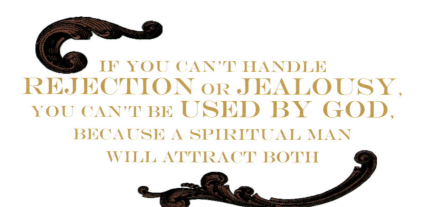

IF YOU CAN'T HANDLE REJECTION OR JEALOUSY, YOU CAN'T BE USED BY GOD, BECAUSE A SPIRITUAL MAN WILL ATTRACT BOTH

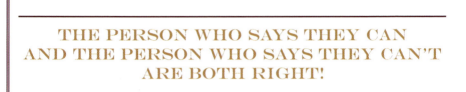

THE PERSON WHO SAYS THEY CAN AND THE PERSON WHO SAYS THEY CAN'T ARE BOTH RIGHT!

### Chapter Fifteen

# FINDINGS FROM DOCTOR WEINER

Dr. Weiner, here in America, walked in to my room the day after he treated my heart condition and told me, "Reverend, you have excellent health!" I asked what he meant and he said "For one thing, none of us believe that you are sixty-three years of age. Your blood pressure is normal; there is no sugar diabetes in your body and there is no cancer in your body. The only thing is this beginning of blockage in the arteries on the outside of the heart."

Dr. Weiner
Dr. Weiner is absolutely brilliant and a total expert in his field!

He went on to say, "What we have done for you is good for over fifty years." My response was, "Doctor, I do not want to be disrespectful, but I don't think I want to hang around in this world another fifty years." He chuckled and together with others he confirmed that what they had done was a smashing success! **TO GOD BE THE GLORY!**

## *Gratitude to Medical Experts and Others*

I give my personal thanks and gratitude to Dr. Jeff Young Jr. and Dr. Weiner for their expertise and total commitment to my recovery and well being. How does one repay such care and love as described herein from strangers, friends, family, and ministers? I am not sure, but my prayers are that the blessings of God be upon all of them. No one is more deserving!

THOSE WHO DO NOT KNOW HOW TO **WEEP** WITH THEIR WHOLE **HEART**, DO NOT KNOW HOW TO **LAUGH** EITHER.

(GOLDA MEIR)

# WE ARE PLUNDERING HELL TO POPULATE HEAVEN!

### Chapter Sixteen

# MY CONTINUING MINISTRY

After a couple of months of rest, I began to travel and preach with more authority than ever before. I feel so excited about the future of my ministry and all that God is going to do for all of us just before His soon return. Soon after I began traveling again, I talked to Brother T.W. Barnes early one morning. He prophesied to me over the phone concerning my future and the happenings of God and this world. Marvelous what is COMING DOWN THE ROAD TOWARD US!

MY MIRACLE ~ AND LIVING THE GOSPEL

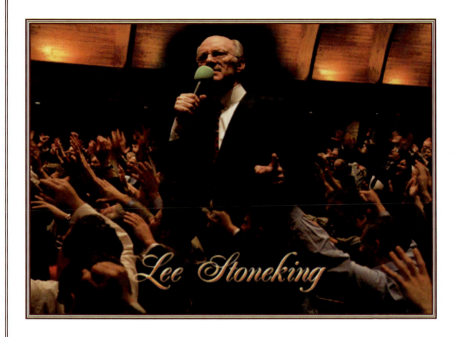

# I shall not die, but live, and declare the works of the Lord.

(Psalm 117:18)

## Understanding:

One truth has become forcefully impressed upon my heart and mind through this ordeal: no matter how many or how few enemies, foes, or demonic powers that war against you, until God says He is through with you, there is neither thing nor force, human or demonic that can touch your life! *GOD IS THE FINAL VOICE AND AUTHORITY IN A CHILD OF GOD'S LIFE* and there is none that can alter it! Those that get in God's way with what He ordains for and with your life will have Him to deal with and will suffer His judgments accordingly. Selah!

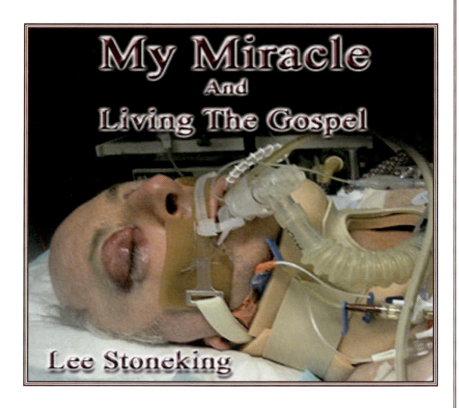

THEY MAY REJECT YOU,
BUT THEY WILL NEVER OUTLIVE
WHAT YOU TOLD THEM...

## Chapter Seventeen

# MY MIRACLE CONTINUES

Return to Australia November 2004

## *Back in Australia One Year Later*

On November 12, 2004, I was once again seated in my normal seating area on the front row of the Campsie church in Sydney. I listened as Brother Slack introduced and welcomed me. When I stood and began walking toward the platform, the audience stood also and gave me a standing ovation.

These folks, having walked through the valley of death with me, knew more than others what it meant to see me alive and with them—once again ready to minister the Word of God. I stepped into the pulpit and said, "Exactly one year ago on November 12, 2003 I dropped dead of a massive heart attack in your airport and was clinically dead for 45 minutes. But tonight I am back, alive and well!" The people continued to stand and to applaud! It was a most emotional moment for me. The Lord manifested His Presence among us that night with a witness of resurrection power! Having been the recipient of that power, I remember feeling a special anointing and love for the saints of God around me.

## *Pieces and Safety Pins*

At the end of the preaching during altar service, we felt a most wonderful and powerful, divine intervention of God. I ministered long to and among those that had gathered there. Then I picked up my Bible making my way to the exit from the sanctuary. A lovely Fijian couple walked toward me. The husband held up a navy sport jacket and said, "This belonged to a dead man." I was struck with recognition and clarity of thought all at the same time. It was the jacket I was wearing when I fell dead on the floor of the airport! But the jacket I now viewed was just large pieces of jacket cloth pinned together with big safety pins. It had been cut from my dead body by the ambulance driver when he came upon my lifeless form lying on the airport restaurant floor. As I stood there looking at it I felt moved with the reality of my miracle of life all over again. He asked, "Do you want it?"

LEE STONEKING

With some kind of urgent force from within I heard myself reply, "Yes!" They explained that they had pinned my jacket together and taken it to the prayer room at the church where people came during all hours of the day and night to gather around it and pray with intercessory prayer for my recovery and total healing! That jacket now hangs in the library of my home, where from time to time I look upon it and reach out touching the pieces, the pins, and recognizing the reality of the Master's Touch upon my otherwise hopeless state. The man's wife explained that her husband had kept my jacket hanging in his closet among his suits and jackets hoping that the anointing in my life and ministry would rub off onto his clothes. I smiled almost tearfully when I heard the story and we chuckled together. Then I breathed a prayer, "Jesus, grant his desire!" The prayer became a part of my sentiment in that most meaningful and appreciative moment. Grateful I am to walk from time to time through the halls of memory surrounding the estate of my death and resurrection. The phrase to *God be the praise and glory* is embedded in my soul for all time. I have a feeling of kinship with biblical figures who tasted death in their lifetimes. Death's bitter aftertaste has been washed away by the Water of Life and finds sweetness from honey in the Rock!

## *Terribly Dead!*

When first admitted to the hospital in Sydney, Brother Nassif used his cell phone to take the following photos. The hospital did not allow anyone to take regular photos but Brother Nassif found a way to take these. I had one photo that I had posted on my website not too long after I returned home in 2003

MY MIRACLE ~ AND LIVING THE GOSPEL

but did not know others existed until returning to Sydney for the conference in 2004. Emotion gripped me and I gasped when he showed me the photos. All I could think of were the words *terribly dead!* Though the photos are small because of the limited camera capabilities of the cell phone, I am forever grateful to Brother Nassif for obtaining this lasting record of my being so *terribly dead*.

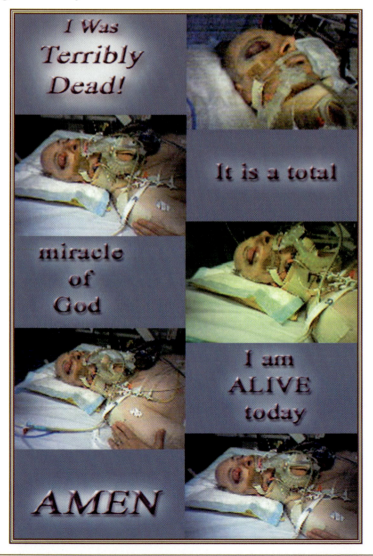

# LEE STONEKING

Airport Restaurant in 2004

## *Back in the Airport Restaurant in 2004*

As we headed for the airport in Sydney after the November 2004 Revival Crusade (one year after the heart attack) I asked Brother Slack if we could have breakfast at the restaurant where I had fallen and lay dead for over thirty minutes the year before. And he replied, "No problem."

In the above photo I am sitting where the policeman, who rushed to assist me with CPR until the ambulance arrived, had been sitting when he saw me fall.

MY MIRACLE ~ AND LIVING THE GOSPEL

The Airport Restaurant Staff

## *The Airport Restaurant Staff Remembers*

They took this picture in November 2004 at the restaurant where I fell dead in 2003. The owner is talking to me and directly behind her to the left is the waitress who recognized us and came running when Bro. Slack and I walked through the door exclaiming as she came, "You look great!"

I simply replied, "I'm doing great! I serve a great God!"

She then went quickly in to the back and brought out the owner who also said, "You look great!" and then she hugged me. They were amazed at the fact that I could return to preach one year later and that I could sit there and laugh, talk and eat breakfast. They remembered the trauma, emotion, and how sad they felt when the medical staff finally carried me away on the stretcher dead.

As we reminisced about the details they told me that the restaurant closed after I fell dead of the heart attack. A crowd gathered around to watch the medical efforts to bring life back into my body — CPR, resuscitation and ten electric shock treatments to my heart. They explained that portable walls were brought and put up to help keep the crowd back.

## *I Have So Many Great Friends!*

When we returned to the airport restaurant, Brother Slack and I were accompanied by Brother and Sister Nassif and Sister Jena Grech. I treasure this photo of the five of us sitting in that restaurant where I positioned myself so that while we ate, I could look just a few feet beyond me and view the floor where one year before I had lain dead for thirty minutes before they placed me on the stretcher and headed to the hospital. The thoughts of God and His power and the reality of His presence washed over me as I sat there with my friends that day. It moved me in ways I cannot totally explain.

MY MIRACLE ~ AND LIVING THE GOSPEL

Pastor Ted Slack and Myself in November 2004

We both know with such reality,

## *WHAT A DIFFERENCE JESUS MAKES!*

He is still the Resurrection and the Life—AMEN!

YOU KNOW WHEN YOU ARE WITH A **TRUE FRIEND**, WHEN **SILENCE** DOES NOT FEEL UNCOMFORTABLE.

## OUR LIFE ONCE STRETCHED NEVER REGAINS THE ORIGINAL DIMENSION
### (OLIVER HOLMES)

## Chapter Eighteen

# DOCTOR PITNEY VIEWS MY RECORDS

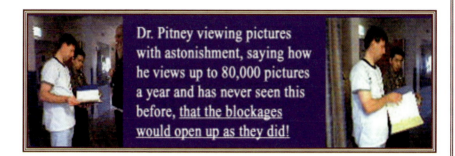

Dr. Pitney viewing pictures with astonishment, saying how he views up to 80,000 pictures a year and has never seen this before, that the blockages would open up as they did!

When I was placed in the ambulance, I was slated for DOA — dead on arrival. I knew shortly after returning to America in 2003 that the blood had coagulated in my hands, forearms, feet and calves. When I returned to Australia in 2004 and talked to Doctor Pitney I learned that the blood had also clotted in my heart. When I began to breathe again and my heart started beating they took pictures and seeing the clotting immediately advised, "We have to cut him open immediately to even try to save his life."

Pastor Slack and those with him replied, "No, we'll pray." After they prayed the doctors took another set of pictures of my heart and the clots and blockages had disappeared!!! So they did not cut me open. The previous photos portray Dr. Pitney's exclamations and comments concerning this miracle.

Dr. Pitney told me himself that there was one huge blood clot at the top of the heart area. But it totally disappeared and he said, "We do not know what happened to it!" **We know what happened! Jesus stepped on the scene!**

Dr. Pitney and I Visit in November 2004

Dr. Pitney and I had a wonderful discussion about it all. He treated me with such kindness and was very interested in my welfare. My reason for going to see him was to simply walk in, shake his hand, and thank him for all he had done for me. He took time to visit with me and gave me the first photos with the clots in my heart and also the second photos without the clots in my heart. They are now in my album of memories from My Miracle in Sydney!

SOMETIMES THE **STRONG** HAVE TO **PROTECT** THOSE WHO CAN'T PROTECT THEMSELVES **NO MATTER** WHAT **THE COST.**

THEY THOUGHT THEY HAD KILLED HIM,
BUT THEY ONLY SET HIM FREE TO LIVE
IN THE HEARTS OF YOU AND ME!

## Chapter Nineteen

# 2004 INTERVIEW WITH THE AMBULANCE DRIVER

Through the year of 2004 before returning to Australia, I stayed in contact with the ambulance driver, Nigel, and asked to see him when I returned in November for the annual meeting in Campsie. He so very kindly agreed and we had lunch together. In all, we spent about three hours chatting and sharing.

During that time I asked him many questions because I knew he was the only person that would know the answers. He attended to me and administered the electric shock treatments to my heart while lying dead on the floor of the Sydney airport. I asked him, "Nigel, what happened when you shocked my heart?" He said, "It would beat two or three times; sometimes four times; and then STOP!"

He further explained, "Lee, everything that could go wrong went wrong. We were not told that you had a heart attack but only that someone had fallen at the airport. This is routine work for us, so we were not aware of the graveness of your situation. People fall daily at the airport resulting in sprains of various kinds."

"It was not until we were walking in the airport that a policeman came and said, 'You must come quickly. This man is very sick. They are giving him CPR.' It was then I realized it was quite serious! When we got to the restaurant and saw you lying on the floor, I knew you were dead. Nothing worked. Even the battery on my machine went dead right in the middle of administering the shock treatments. I had not been able to recharge the battery after the last call. Everything that could go wrong went wrong. Even though I did not know you had a heart attack and I knew that my battery was almost dead, for some reason I felt to bring my machine in to the airport when I came."

He explained that another paramedic had come to the scene and she also had felt to bring her machine with her. "The machines were interchangeable," Nigel explained, "Even though it took just a few seconds, it seemed endless before we got reconnected to the shock procedure."

I asked, "Nigel, when did I really begin to breathe and my heart begin to beat?" You are the only one that would know.

He answered, "Lee, it was not until you were in the ambulance on the way to the hospital and expected to arrive DOA — dead on arrival."

I asked, "So, Nigel, I was actually clinically dead for longer than thirty minutes wasn't I?"

He replied immediately, "Lee, you were dead for at least forty-five minutes."

At that point I understood that my condition was far worse than I realized and the miracle of being raised from the dead even more miraculous than I had understood!

## *Motivation to Preach As Never Before*

How can I repay Jesus, Nigel, doctors, Pastor Slack and congregation there in Sydney and the believers worldwide for all they have so graciously done? My only recourse is continuing on behalf of Jesus Christ in obeying the Great Commission to preach the Gospel to every creature. It is all I know and feel to do.

Observing the anointed difference in my preaching and the might of God's demonstrative Power accompanying it since my resurrection experience, someone said, "What a price to pay for the difference!"

 MY MIRACLE ~ AND LIVING THE GOSPEL

My reply: **"BEHOLD THE PURCHASE OF SUCH A PRICE!"** For I have received phone calls and letters stating that the faith for the miraculous had almost been lost among us in some areas of the country until they read and/or heard my testimony of being raised from the dead by the Hand of the Lord! Miraculous healings have taken place in the lives of people all over the world where I have gone since I have been raised from the dead!

His every wish is my command and someday when I see Him, my ultimate reward will be to simply hear Him say: **"WELL DONE."** Nothing else really matters to me. Likewise for all those who stand before Him on that great day, every ear will be straining to hear the same two words, **"WELL DONE!"**

I LOVE YOU BECAUSE
OF WHAT YOU ARE, BUT I LOVE YOU
MOST FOR WHAT I AM
WHEN I AM WITH YOU…

## Chapter Twenty

# THANKS TO THE AUSTRALIAN CHURCH

The sacrifices of love and devotion shown and demonstrated by the Australian church staff and people during my hospital vigil are indelibly engrained in my memory. I can never forget. They sat with me daily and through the nights. They never left me alone but continuously prayed to God on my behalf. The power of prayer by the people of God has no equal. In the church we are covered with that which moves the heart, the might, and the Hand of God!

THE MORE YOU KNOW WHO YOU ARE,
THE LESS YOU CARE HOW
PEOPLE VIEW YOU!

## Chapter Twenty-one

# RETURN FOR MEDICAL EXAM IN MARCH 2007

In March of 2007, I returned to the Jackson, Tennessee area for an annual crusade with Rev. Jeff Young. During this tenure of duty, I returned to Dr. Weiner and Dr. Young for a complete blood lipid profile. The profile was to include; cholesterol, HDLS, LDLS, and triglycerides. Since I am on no medication of any kind, I was interested in seeing what my blood lipid status would be. Six vials of blood were drawn and sent to Oakland, California for analysis. A period of two weeks is required to process the results. With my travel schedule, I was unable to make contact for the results until three weeks later.

## *DNA Results—Most Unusual!*

When I called Doctor Young and he heard my voice, he began laughing. I said, "What are you laughing at?" He said, "You." I said, "Why?" He said, "We take hundreds of these blood samples daily — your results are the best we have seen!" Dr. Jeff Young Jr then proceeded to tell me the most interesting information that I had heard to date and I quote him: "We can now check a person's DNA. We decided to check yours. The results: We found that you are not carrying the APOE geno genetic marker for heart disease! When God raised you from the dead, He removed it! This cannot be done! A miracle totally! Only God could do such a thing!"

## *Priceless Truth Has Become Part of Me*

That I am alive and well is a total miracle of God! The most valuable and deep priceless truth and understanding that one could be given in this life comes to me on a continual daily basis:

 I was instantaneously and suddenly gone – dead in a second with no warning.

 I am reminded that I do not have the past – the past is gone forever.

 I understand that I do not have the future – it is not here yet.

 I am aware that **<u>all I have is this moment in time!</u>**

Some people spend a lifetime living in the past. Others spend a lifetime living in the future – in so doing, they miss the present! I realize I could be dead in the next second. All I have is this moment in time, so I make the best of this moment. This knowledge brings freedom to me that makes each moment more meaningful than before. I am happy in my now – it is all I have.

## *Conclusion*

May you also enter into this paradise of reality and live as the Creator intended. In so doing, the possessor of eternity you will become! God bless all who read here and may the reality of God and your life now flood your whole being as never before! Jesus, grant it I pray!

Alive In Him,

*Lee Stoneking*